seaside tinker treasures

seaside tinkered treasures

35 simple projects to bring the seashore home

Elyse Major

Foreword by Selina Lake

CICO BOOKS

LONDON NEW YORK

For my mom and dad,
Joyce Epstein Crossley
and Allan Press.

Published in 2014 by CICO Books
An imprint of Ryland Peters & Small
519 Broadway, 5th Floor,
New York NY 10012
20–21 Jockey's Fields,
London WC1R 4BW

www.rylandpeters.com

Text © Elyse Major 2014
Design, photography, and
illustration © CICO Books 2014

A CIP catalog record for this book is
available from the Library of
Congress and the British Library.

ISBN: 978-1-78249-087-6

contents

Foreword

As an interiors stylist and author myself, I was delighted to be asked to write the foreword for this book. In a similar way to Elyse, I love to share my homespun styling ideas and create little makes from items I already have and from secondhand pieces I find along the way. Elyse shared the theme for her second craft book with me in the spring of 2013, when I had the pleasure of meeting her in person after being Facebook and blogging friends for a while. I thought her *Seaside Tinkered Treasures* idea sounded delightful. Being by the seaside has always inspired me and, like many people, I can't resist collecting a few pebbles, shells, and driftwood when I visit the coast. How great it is that Elyse has so many ideas for ways that we can tinker our own treasures. I certainly can't wait to give the grocery bag bunting and rustic windchime a go!

So back to that sunny spring morning in Spring when Elyse and I arranged to meet in London at the Columbia Road Flower Market. She was in the UK promoting her debut book *Tinkered Treasures*. It was lovely to see her; we swapped our new books with each other, drank English tea, and chatted about all things crafty.

Congratulations to my new friend Elyse on producing another inspiring book.

Selina Lake
Interior stylist and author of *Pretty Pastel Style*
www.selinalake.blogspot.com

Introduction

For as long as I can remember I have been smitten with beach cottages—not the opulent new-construction houses with tall views of the ocean but old, non-winterized types furnished frugally with simple odds and ends. Small, modest places that conjure up images of beds made with floral sheets, soft and faded from years of use, where sun-bleached towels hang by the back door on a row of weathered hooks, and woven baskets dangle at the ready to serve blueberry muffins when not adding rustic charm to walls.

Like many, I have fond memories of summertime that I bring to my mind's eye for warmth and peace on cooler, busier days: mental snapshots of striped umbrellas dotting stretches of beachfront, picnic lunches laced with gritty sand despite our best efforts, and amusingly quirky roadside souvenirs fashioned from seashells.

Welcome to *Seaside Tinkered Treasures*, my second craft book which builds upon the premise of transforming everyday nothings into wonderful somethings introduced in my first book *Tinkered Treasures*. Each project in this book has been designed to channel the relaxed state of a summer by the sea through endeavors that will have you making whimsical accents to decorate your place in the sun, cheerfully and resourcefully.

I would like you to think of this book as a sort of guidebook for a never-ending, all-ages summer camp. Most materials are things you either might already have or are not difficult to find and the projects are just as uncomplicated. Whether you have fresh sand in your sneakers or snow caked beneath your boots, the makes found within these pages aim to become prized tokens of bright, pleasant times spent creating.

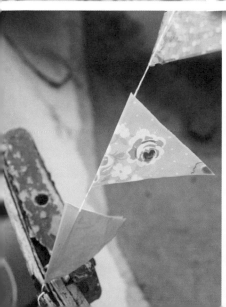

GETTING STARTED

Most projects in this book have very humble beginnings: a box of pasta, piles of craft sticks, and handfuls of seashells. What will change these items into unique home accents are the light touches you add to them—such as a paper rose, a sparkling gem, or a scrap of favorite fabric. Each project has a list of what you will need divided into two groups: materials and tools. Materials itemizes the supplies you will need to gather for each project; the Tools for Tinkering section lists things like glue and scissors. Some projects offer a Tinker Tip as a helpful resource, and Fancy This is meant as a suggested alternative for the project or its intended use. The techniques that I have used are simple and unchallenging—anyone can tinker!

Materials

Begin to save and collect a supply of things for tinkering times, perhaps keeping them in a photo or shoebox that you decorate with paper and fabric scraps into your very own box of treasures. These are some of the things you will be using to tinker. Remember that the projects here illustrate my personal palette and motif preferences but can easily be altered to what suits your style or the season best with simple switches in color, pattern, and paper.

Adhesive gems: Available in a variety of sizes, find flat-backed gems in finishes from metal to pearl to rhinestone. When using on rough surfaces, such as ridged shells or coarse sand, fix in place with craft glue in addition to the adhesive backing.

Baker's twine: Twisted strands of two colors make baker's twine a cheerful way to add seaside striping to projects that call for hanging or tying.

Corsage pins (pearl-headed dressmaker's pins): Longer than usual pins (2½ in /5 cm), these often have decorative or pear-shaped heads.

Craft sticks: Wooden craft sticks, often referred to as popsicle (lolly) sticks, come in the standard 6 in (15 cm) size as well as smaller sizes. These round-edged, flat sticks are cheap and take easily to glue and paint, making them a perennial crafting favorite. When projects call for sticks to line up neatly, avoid curved or bent pieces—instead save those for stirring paint.

Embroidery floss (thread): Low cost and a wide assortment of colors make this cotton thread perfect for creating Merpeg hair (see page 113).

Fabric: The fabrics used in this book are all cotton quilting fabrics—I've either used them as they are or scanned or photocopied them to create pretty paper (see page 16).

Millinery forget-me-nots: A favorite! Flocked bunches of dainty flowers and blossoms, generally found in twelve floral sprigs on paper-wrapped wire stems, add delightful bursts of color to any project. Seek these vintage items in specialty or old craft or fabric stores, or from online retailers.

Paint chips: The paper cards of related shades displayed alongside paint. The sturdiness, color variety, and fact that they are usually offered free-of-charge, work together to make this supply virtually risk-free for tinkering experimentation. Use tact when taking cards or your local paint vendor is likely to shoo you away.

Paper roses: Small roses made of paper can be found twisted in wired clusters or with adhesive backing. Use to adorn projects instantly and take them to new levels of loveliness.

SCAVENGER HUNT

Look around your home for things that could serve you well to add flourishes to projects.

• Small envelopes filled with extra buttons that are sometimes attached to new garments

• Tall pins from a corsage

• Colorful amusement-ride ticket stubs

• Travel brochures and take-out menus

• Broken jewelry

• Unique gift packaging

When you stroll through home improvement and craft stores, markets, and more always consider the possible alternative uses of what you see.

A ceramic planter becomes a vase to hold cropped bunches of flowers

A one-off valance becomes a table runner

Chipped china dishes become an unexpected garden border when partially submerged along flowerbeds

A ruffled shower curtain becomes a tablecloth

Sea glass: No luck finding sea glass along the ocean? Purchase a pack from a craft supplier. Best spots for finding sea glass are unkempt, littered beaches.

Seashells: Bags of shells in a wide variety of assortments can be purchased at craft stores and from online retailers. If gathering shells from the ocean, be sure they are emptied of sea life and sand, and give them a soak in a 50/50 mix of bleach and water overnight followed by a good rinse in water, or place carefully in the top rack of a dishwasher and run with a regular load of dishes. Other sources for shells are the fish market and seafood restaurants.

Ribbon: When you find "ribbon" in a project list, the choice is yours from grosgrain to satin, patterned or plain, wide or narrow. My very favorite ribbon to work with is seam binding for its thin and pliable weight, often found in soft sherbet shades. Like millinery forget-me-nots, seek this vintage item in specialty or old craft or fabric stores, or from online retailers.

Vials: Small bottles found in laboratories are now sold with scrapbooking supplies.

Tools for tinkering

Most projects in this book begin with a sharp pair of scissors and a bottle of craft glue. Seek many tried-and-true provisions alongside school supplies and stock up when things are on clearance just after a new semester has started.

GLUE

Craft/school: Easy to find, white glue that dries quickly and is generally non-toxic. Apply sparingly in thin lines or small dots to ensure fast dry-time. Best for wood, fabric, and heavy stock paper.

Decoupage medium: Refers to an all-in-one glue, sealer, and finish. It is possible to make decoupage medium by mixing equal parts of white craft/school glue and water (test results on scrap paper before using). It is used in the traditional sense, to stick and then seal small, cut-out images to larger objects but also as a way of sealing projects to make them watertight, such as in the Sea-glass Mosaic Frame (see page 54).

Glue stick: Preferred for paper to avoid dampening sometimes caused by white craft/school glue. For best results apply in broad, light strokes.

Hot glue gun: Ideal for joining heavier and porous items, such as shells, sticks, and stones, and attaching assembled pieces together, like the panels of the Craft Stick Cottage (see page 106). When using hot glue, read all instructions and guidelines and use with caution to avoid burns. A benefit to using hot glue for projects like the Craft Stick Cottage is that you have a brief period to make adjustments before the glue sets and that there is not a lengthy period of waiting for glue to dry and set.

Glue pen: For applying very thin strokes of glue, look for a fine point glue pen or dip a toothpick into glue.

PAINT

Acrylic/craft paint: Available in a multitude of colors, varied finishes like satin or high-gloss, and made for different uses like applying to wood or metal.

Latex paint: In addition to using home project leftovers, purchase tintable tester-sized containers (7.75 fl oz/229 ml) of interior latex in white base and select your favorite color(s) from literally thousands of paint chips. You can even have your paint color-matched to your favorite paper and/or fabric.

Spray paint: Can be used on wood, metal, ceramic, and more. Be sure to follow the manufacturer's directions and use outdoors during calm, dry weather for best results. Use spray paint for covering intricate surfaces thoroughly or many pieces at once.

PAINTBRUSHES

Foam brushes: Inexpensive and readily available at craft and home improvement stores, foam brushes are perfect for applying decoupage medium, latex, and craft paint.

Bristle paintbrushes: A small or medium paintbrush (size 8) is handy for painting smaller and singular items, such as pasta shapes or craft sticks.

PAPER PLATES

Just sturdy enough, pliable, and recyclable, paper plates make terrific palettes for paint. Use them when sprinkling glitter—not only to contain mess but to then roll and funnel to return excess glitter to containers.

PAPER PUNCHES

Hand-held hole punches are perfect for making round openings from tiny to small. For larger shapes, try a decorative punch found in shapes such as scalloped circles and even sand dollars. Try an edger punch for making continuous lace and floral-like patterns.

SCISSORS

For best results, use a sharp pair of scissors for cutting and trimming—it's a good idea to have a separate pair for paper and fabric. For decorative details such as scalloped finishes, use pattern-edged scissors or pinking shears.

WAX PAPER

Found in the supermarket near parchment paper and foil, wax paper is my go-to for protecting a work area. Easy to tear off the roll in any size, wax paper is semi-translucent, which keeps it from being dark and distracting. Wax paper is also moisture-proof, making it the perfect choice when working with glue and paint.

Techniques

Here are a few of the basic methods used for the projects in this book—all very unchallenging and fun to do. For any techniques not covered here, consult reputable online sources, such as product websites and craft encyclopedias, or the instructions given by the manufacturer of your supplies.

Making pretty paper and pretty labels

Some of the paper pictured in the projects that follow, such as the bold striped paper, are decorative scrapbooking papers but many of them use what I refer to as "pretty paper"—color copies of my favorite fabrics. All you need is some offcuts of pretty fabric and access to a color copier or printer.

MATERIALS
Favorite fabrics (cotton quilting fabrics work best)
Printer paper, letter size multipurpose
Cardstock (optional)
Standard 1 x 2⅝ in (2.5 x 6.5 cm) mailing labels, white, 30 labels per sheet

TOOLS
Iron and ironing board
Scanner and color printer or color copier

1 Find beautiful fabrics that make your heart race. Begin by sorting through a stash of cotton fabric remnants, borrow fabric from a friend, or purchase small quantities like "fat quarter" bundles. Pieces do not need to be any larger than letter size paper and will not be damaged.

2 Using the correct temperature for your fabric, iron out any creases. Determine if you will scan fabrics at home or bring to a copy center to print in color. If making pretty labels, you will need to scan fabrics.

3 Place one fabric at a time neatly on the glass of a scanner or copier, avoiding any folds. Print as-is or experiment with adjusting settings to reduce or enlarge, light or dark, low or high contrast. A single piece of fabric can look vastly different after print settings have been changed.

4 Use standard paper for most projects but also copy a small supply onto white or ivory cardstock for tinkering heavier-weight items. You now have an inventory of custom pretty paper for tinkering!

5 For pretty labels, scan the fabric avoiding any folds. Experiment with adjusting settings until your image is how you want it to be: reduced or enlarged, darker or lighter, high or low contrast, or as-is.

6 Scanned images should be "Saved As" in a format that can be uploaded (Jpeg, for instance) into a label template. Sound complicated? Photograph fabrics instead.

7 Upload the fabric images into a mailing label template. You may need to adjust the size of your image to fit in each label field.

8 Consider overlaying a text box that has "no fill" and "no outline" and type in words or phrases over the images.

9 Print the design on an adhesive mailing label sheet. You now have 30 pretty labels to use as you desire!

TINKER TIPS Make multiple copies of your very favorite fabrics as pretty paper to have handy for repeated use and for projects that require more than one sheet of paper.

Use remnants of pretty labels in place of paper strips and glue for smaller projects that call for scraps, or substitute for tape.

Enlarge favorite motifs, such as rose clusters, to use on larger projects.

Instead of fabric, copy wallpaper samples, patterned napkins, a pillowcase.

FANCY THIS Coordinate projects to match rooms, fabric gifts, and more.

Other paper options include newspaper, giftwrap, old book pages, photocopied album covers, greeting cards, and photographs.

Trimming motifs

Many projects in this book call for cutting a motif or an image from paper. Choosing to cut challenging images, such as intricate clusters of roses and their petals, can be arduous but with a bit of practice you'll be up for the challenge!

1 Begin by cutting your chosen image within a tight square.

2 Next, get even closer by cutting straight lines from point to point followed by snipping away any triangles.

3 To get really close in, hold the paper with your non-dominant hand and slowly steer and turn the image while cutting with scissors in your dominant hand.

STEP 1

STEP 2

STEP 3

TINKER TIP If you accidentally snip off a small piece such as a leaf, simply reposition it to the main portion once glued onto the project surface.

Tearing paper and fabric

If precision cutting is not for you, tear paper or fabric instead of cutting with scissors to give projects a slightly tattered quality. The frayed edge of the fabric will add seaside charm to your projects. For paper, simply cut small squares or tear pieces and place in seemingly random order to create collages on projects. Substitute cut images with stickers if you prefer.

1 For fabric, cut a small snip (about 1 in/2.5 cm) at an edge and slowly tear in two; the fabric will have a frayed edge (which I like) and will be accurately cut along the grain.

2 For paper, tear into desired sizes.

Decoupage

To decoupage is to cut images from paper, adhere to something, and then seal with layers of finish. For the projects in this book that require decoupage, you will see decoupage medium in the materials list which refers to products like Mod Podge®, an all-in-one glue, sealer, and finish. Avoid getting decoupaged items wet.

1 First gather the paper pieces you wish to adhere to your surface. If you plan to cut an image from patterned paper, refer to Trimming Motifs (page 18) for tips. Once ready with your paper cut-outs, pour a small amount of decoupage medium onto a paper plate.

2 Lightly brush or stipple (make small dots) decoupage medium to the back of your cut image or apply glue stick, and gently position on the surface of your project and press to fix in place.

3 Brush a light coat of decoupage medium over the image using a dry foam brush. Cover the entire top-surface for a consistent finish all over.

4 Smooth any wrinkles gently with your fingers, either after a few minutes or immediately using direct heat from a blow dryer.

5 Let dry and then continue to add coats of decoupage medium, allowing to dry in-between coats until you have the finish you want. When finished, rinse the foam brush until water runs clear and squeeze dry to use again.

STEP 2

STEP 3

Using glue

Large amounts of glue are not usually needed to get the job done—in fact, heavy applications of glue will slow down your project due to the lengthy time needed for drying. Choosing the correct glue for the material is also key for good results.

1 Always be sure to apply sparingly in thin lines or small dots.

2 My method of glue stick application is to begin at the center of the paper and move away in all directions, as if drawing rays of sunshine.

3 For applying to braid, run the glue stick lightly along the reverse of the braid. Be careful not to get glue on the front surface.

4 For applying very thin strokes of glue for glitter application, look for a fine point glue pen or dip a toothpick into glue.

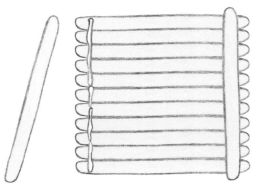

STEP 1

STEP 3

STEP 4

chapter 1
tinkering beachy bits & bobs

You'll truly feel like you're away at summer camp—minus the bug spray and sun tan lotion—with a series of breezy projects that will have you tearing old beach towels, festooning flip-flops, and playing with sand. With supply lists that read like items on a scavenger hunt, find yourself foraging for sticks, searching for shells, reaching for stars, and smiling.

beach ball vase fillers

Layer strips of faded fabrics and sherbet-hued ribbons over Styrofoam balls to create a delightful summertime accent. A subtle nod to brightly paneled beach balls, these soft and fetching counterparts will bring an air of buoyancy to any space. Corral a bunch in a basket or vase for a playful vignette.

MATERIALS
Strips of cotton fabric, ribbon, or seam binding
Styrofoam balls

TOOLS
Scissors
Craft glue

TINKER TIP If you choose to wrap balls with materials that are heavy in weight, sturdy or with a shine finish, you may need to use a glue gun instead of craft glue.

FANCY THIS Attach a long strip of fabric or ribbon to one axis using a corsage pin and then hang the balls from places like chandelier arms as a pretty decoration.

1 Gather together ribbon and fabric strips that are narrow and long enough to wrap around the circumference of your Styrofoam ball once—choose materials that are lightweight and pliable so that they can be glued easily, such as vintage seam binding. For fabric strips, simply snip the edge of a piece of fabric and slowly tear to make a straight but frayed strip. Trim any excessive threads. If you prefer more of a refined look, cut strips with sharp scissors; or use pinking shears to add interest.

2 Begin by wrapping the ball with a first strip of fabric/ribbon; fix with a dot of craft glue and press gently to secure. (The first couple of wraps may not be visible as the ball gets covered with additional strips.)

3 Once the first strip is in place, add another that crosses over it in a plus-sign pattern. Use the section where the first two strips intersect as an imaginary base or axis. Continue to add strips, wrapping them diagonally and making sure they lie flat and tight. Alternate where you begin and end the strips so that one end doesn't become too thick.

4 Continue to add strips until the ball is completely covered and you can no longer see the Styrofoam underneath. Stick down any loose pieces with glue and allow to dry thoroughly. Display!

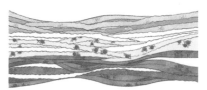

STEP 1

STEP 2

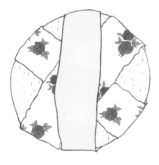

STEP 3

marine antoinette and troupe

Sift through an assortment of shells to uncover personalities just waiting to take shape. Perhaps you'll picture a freckled face on a brown and white ark clam shell or dress a figurine in a delicate shell dress. Enjoy putting your imprint on this reimagined version of a tourist trap favorite.

MATERIALS
Assorted shells (see right)
Chenille sticks (pipe cleaners)
Small starfish
Faux pearls or small shell, to embellish
Sand dollar or pansy shell and toothpick (optional)

TOOLS
Aluminum foil to protect your work surface
Hot glue gun
Permanent fine point markers

• This project calls for real seashells, which you can find in a number of ways: collecting them from the shore, saving them from a seafood dinner, inquiring at your local fish market, or purchasing assorted shells at craft shops or online.
• Whenever you use seashells that you have found, be sure to rinse off the sand and clean them either by soaking them in a mixture of 50/50 bleach and water or by running them through the dishwasher (see Seashells, page 13).
• Whatever shells you are able to find, use the pictures as your guide. Start by assembling a sturdy base resembling a skirt and build up from there.
• For best results, use a hot glue gun for rapid adhesion. Protect your work surface with something heat resistant, such as aluminum foil.

1 Find two large shells that look as if they could be a pair and join them where they would meet with the hot glue gun; pull them slightly apart so they are able to work together to stand.

2 Take another pair of shells, ideally slightly smaller and in a different color, and attach to the top; turn them so that they are going in the opposite direction. It should start to look like a skirt with a bustle. You can add another pair of smaller shells to further decorate, if desired.

TINKER TIP Drawing features over the rigid lines of a seashell can be challenging so mark small strokes instead. Consider practicing on another shell first.

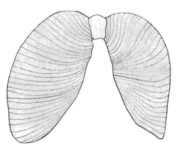

STEP 1

STEP 2

3 Glue a cowrie shell upright to the center. This will act as the short body. Cut a section of chenille stick (pipe cleaner) approximately 6 in (15 cm) long and bend in half; bend a bit at each end to make little hands and to secure any sharp wire edges. Hot glue the center of the chenille stick around the back of the standing cowrie shell and then bend and shape until secure around the doll as arms.

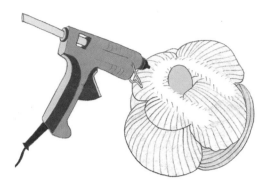

STEP 3

4 Glue a small white (ark clam) shell to the base of a billowy (whelk) shell to resemble a face and tall, elaborate hairdo. Draw a face onto the white shell using permanent markers—you may want to practice on paper first. I find the simpler the face, the better, as the ridge of the shell can be challenging to mark.

STEP 4

5 Once you are happy with the head, either hot glue it directly to the top of the standing cowrie shell or place a small starfish between the face and body first.

6 Hot glue an accessory into one or both of her hands, for example a small flat brown shell can be positioned to look like a fan. To make a parasol, hot glue a toothpick into the natural hole beneath a sand dollar or pansy shell.

STEP 5

beachcomber accessories

Bring home the natural beauty of the beach with accoutrements sure to keep you happy as a clam. With subtle modifications, larger shallow shells easily become jewelry trays and ring holders, while smaller versions with organic holes lend themselves to being outfitted with ribbon to adorn bottles of sand or to be worn as necklaces.

MATERIALS

Clam shells of all sizes
Fabric scraps
Embellishments such as cabochons, paper roses, and pearly beads
Pretty paper (see page 16) or paper flower motifs
Ribbon, seam binding, baker's twine

TOOLS

Paint (acrylic craft or spray)
Paper plate as palette for paint and decoupage medium
Foam brush
Craft glue
Decoupage medium
Wax paper to protect your work surface

1 Make sure your seashells are clean and dry (see Seashells, page 13). To create jewelry trays from the larger shells, start by painting the shell—either one or both sides as desired. Use acrylic paint and a dry foam brush for a lighter wash of color or spray paint for full coverage. Trace around the outer shell onto fabric and cut out the shape. Trim to fit and snip at intervals around the edges to help the fabric fit the curves once placed inside the shell.

2 To make a pedestal version—perfect for holding your precious rings by the sink—position a larger shell on top of a smaller one and use a hot glue gun to secure.

3 Paint smaller shells in the same way but this time decorate them with small floral motifs. Apply a coat of decoupage medium and allow to dry.

4 Add tiny beads or gems to decorate the shells and secure with craft glue. Many small clam shells already have a natural hole toward the top; slip a length of twine or ribbon through this for hanging.

STEP 1

STEP 2

STEP 3

STEP 4

TINKER TIP If the shell you want to hang doesn't have a hole already, wrap it in a web of string or piable wire, or try using a small drill.

FANCY THIS Before tidying up your craftermath, play with creating with seashells and notions. Glue a section of fused beads where a bivalve shell connects and add two bits of baker's twine to create a butterfly or get out the googly eyes to make silly little creatures.

pier mirror

Small spaces call for furnishings that serve multiple functions, like this wall accent that is memory board and mirror all in one. Hang to cast light and movement into any space while reflecting on memos as you prep for the day. A scrap of fabric clipped to two top clothespins serves as a pretty hanger.

MATERIALS

Unfinished wood-framed mirror (available at craft stores)
Wooden clothespins, with springs
Fabric
Pretty paper (see page 16)

TOOLS

Pencil and ruler (optional)
Hot glue gun or wood glue
Decoupage medium
Paper plate as palette
Paint (acrylic craft, latex, or spray) in your chosen base color and white
Foam brush
Scissors
Glue stick
Wax paper to protect your work surface

TINKER TIP Avoid hanging items that are very heavy—postcards and scraps of paper are ideal.

FANCY THIS Paint the wood frame first and then stick on your own tinkered clothespins (see Beach Towel Table Set, page 36, for suggestions on how to decorate).

1 For best results, carefully remove the mirror prior to working on this project and return when completed.

2 Begin by determining where you will be placing clothespins on the mirror frame, either by eyeing the distance or measuring and then marking lightly with a pencil, if needed. Using a hot glue gun or wood glue, affix a row of clothespins to the top of the mirror with their clasps pointed up, followed by a row of clothespins to the bottom of the mirror with their clasps pointed down. Allow to dry and set well.

3 Unify the clothespins and wooden frame by painting them all the same color using a foam brush. Here, I applied a coat of pale pink first, followed by an imperfect coat of white.

4 Trim floral motifs from your pretty paper and stick them down the sides of the frame using glue stick. Seal with a coat of decoupage medium and allow to dry.

5 Tear a strip of fabric approximately 12 in (30 cm) long and clip it to the two top outer clothespins for hanging.

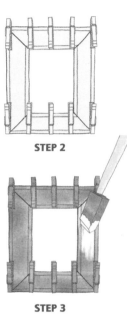

STEP 2

STEP 3

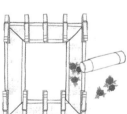

STEP 4

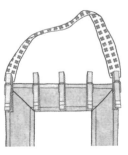

STEP 5

rustic windchime

Conjure the calming sounds of a summer night anytime with this rustic chic accessory made from natural elements. Enjoy the process of gathering what you need before turning it all into something wonderful and unique. Use as an indoor windchime or alluring wall accent sure warmly to convert any draft into a melodic sea breeze.

MATERIALS
Branch, stick, or driftwood
Ribbon
Fabric strips
Seashells, sea glass

TOOLS
Paint (spray, acrylic craft, or latex)
Paintbrush (optional)
Hot glue gun

1 Locate a fallen branch, stick, or piece of driftwood that is the size you like, or carefully snap to size. Be sure that the stick is dry and sturdy. Give the stick a light coat of paint so that a bit of the natural wood grain shows through. Allow to dry.

2 Gather together your "chimes" and prepare as desired: you may wish to paint seashells, leave them natural, or have some of both; use pieces of sea glass; even large beads.

3 Take a selection of fabric strips and lengths of ribbon and start securing a chime piece to the end of each one. Bonding with a hot glue gun is fast and secure but you could also use craft glue, or even wrap the items securely with strips of ribbon.

4 Tie one extra-long fabric strip or ribbon to each end of the branch and use to hang up. Tie each fabric strip or ribbon to the branch and then use short strips of fabric or ribbon to tie small bows close to the dangling element for added prettiness.

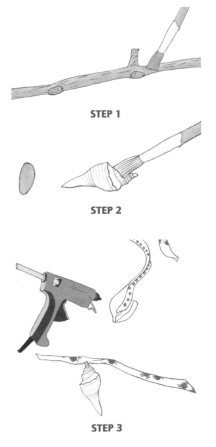

STEP 1

STEP 2

STEP 3

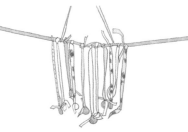

STEP 4

TINKER TIP For best results, use indoors.

beach towel table set

Bring all the fun of dining on the beach to your table with a collection of linens fabricated from a well-worn beach towel. Rip nubby cloth into a soft, carefree set that includes a runner and napkins. Add starfish to narrow fabric strips for napkin rings and weight the edges with clothespins to finish a sunny ensemble that's sure to make waves.

MATERIALS
Beach towel
Fabric
Starfish, real or resin
Paper flowers, gems, or small seashells
Wooden clothespins, with springs
Pretty paper (see page 16)

TOOLS
Scissors
Hot glue gun
Spray paint
Glue stick
Decoupage medium
Foam brush
Paper plate as palette
Wax paper to protect your work surface

1 Start with a beach towel that is clean and dry. Lay the towel flat on a table or the floor and determine where you will cut and rip the runner. As this will be the largest and most visible section, choose the best part of the towel, avoiding any holes. Next, cut a snip through any heavy banding until you get to the terry cloth and then put the scissors down and tear the fabric along the length. Repeat until you have a wide table runner with two long frayed edges.

2 For napkins, review what is left of your towel to determine the size your napkins should be. Base their shape on a square and cut and rip squares until you have a small set.

STEP 1

STEP 2

3 For napkin rings, rip longer scraps into strips. Leave them as they are or decorate them by hot-gluing a spray-painted starfish or seashell to the center of the strip. Tear strips of fabric wider than the napkin rings and glue or simply position beneath to add a layered effect to the gathered napkins. Further embellish by hot-gluing a paper flower, gem, or small shell to the center of the starfish.

4 Spray-paint clothespins and decorate with scraps of fabric or paper that have been trimmed to fit. Simply affix with glue stick and apply a coat of decoupage medium to seal. Clip to the hanging edges of the table runner to work as weights to keep the cloth from blowing about.

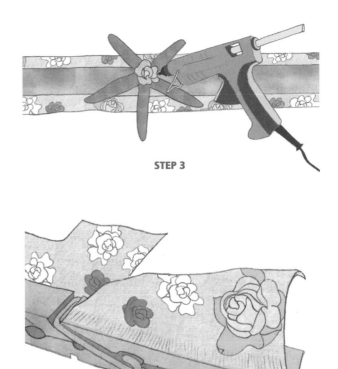

STEP 3

STEP 4

FANCY THIS Keep this set at the ready by storing in a just-as-worn and faded pillowcase: lay a pillowcase flat with the closed side at the bottom; clip the two sides together at the top in the center and, keeping about 3 in (8 cm) together, cut two sloping lines away and down to the side creases so that the pillowcase resembles a pizza-paddle shape. Finally, remove the clip, and snip and tie at the top.

beach hut birdhouse

Be happier than a seagull with a crumb when you make over a plain birdhouse into a chirpy cabana. Easy-to-find small birdhouses made of wood or papier mâché readily take to remodeling. Add seaside stripes and a cocktail umbrella for an amusing accent that harkens back to the early days of beach-going.

MATERIALS

Birdhouse meant for crafting
Striped scrapbooking paper
Pretty paper (see page 16)
Fabric scraps
Fabric trimming such as baby pompom fringe or daisy fabric trimming
Cocktail umbrella

TOOLS

Scissors
Craft glue
Decoupage medium (optional)
Foam brush
Paper plate as palette
Toothpick
Glue stick
Wax paper to protect your work surface

TINKER TIP For indoor use only.

FANCY THIS Display on a tray filled with sand and seashells or place in front of postcards and images depicting vintage seaside resorts for a Victorian-inspired vignette.

1 Working in small and easy to manage sections, trim pieces of striped paper to fit the panels of the birdhouse. You can do this by tracing, measuring, and then cutting or by gluing pieces first and then trimming. You can even press paper over the shape to create folds and creases and then use these as cutting guidelines. The stripes will help you cut straight lines. Once you have glued on all the pieces you may wish to add light coats of decoupage medium, rubbing it into the seams to seal to the birdhouse.

2 Make a flag for the top of your beach hut by folding a rectangle of pretty paper in half and then trimming to a pointed flag shape. Place the fold over a toothpick and use glue stick to secure. Snip or break off the opposite point and then glue the flat edge of the toothpick to the roof using craft glue. Use the same paper someplace else to add interest, such as a small windowsill.

3 Glue strips of fabric to each section of the roof to serve as a decorative overhang or awning. Glue a short section of trimming around the flagpole and a band of trimming around the base of the beach hut. Finally, tuck a cocktail umbrella into the base trimming.

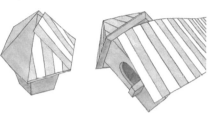

STEP 1

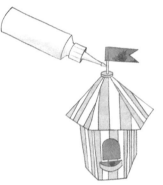

STEP 2

STEP 3

sandcastle birdhouse

Make a lasting impression when you convert a stark birdhouse into a decorative sandcastle. Capture the sparkle of a glorious day by the sea by adding glitter and an assemblage of luminous findings. Display wherever you most need reminding of sun-filled days with sand between your toes.

MATERIALS

Sand
Glitter
Birdhouse meant for crafting
Small seashells and related objects
Embellishments: beads, cabochons, gems, sequins

TOOLS

Paper plates as palette and glitter and sand tray
Decoupage medium
Foam brush
Craft glue
Hot glue gun (optional)
Wax paper to protect your work surface

1 Please note that this project can be messy and even once completed, sand may settle and fall. To add glitter to the sand, simply pour some sand into a paper plate and stir in some glitter. Alternatively you could sprinkle the glitter over the birdhouse once you have covered it with sand.

2 Begin by brushing the entire birdhouse with a layer of decoupage medium, using a foam brush. For smaller areas that are harder to reach, skip the foam brush and use your finger.

3 Cover the birdhouse with sand— start by laying the birdhouse in your sand-filled paper plate and sprinkling with sand and then turn to repeat on the other sides. Shake to reveal any missed spots and repeat as needed.

STEP 1

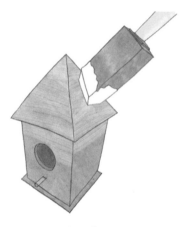

STEP 2

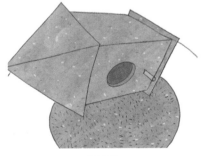

STEP 3

TINKER TIP If you don't have sand, use tinted salt (see Hurricane Candle Holder, page 124). The project shown was made using embellishments of a limited color range of aqua and blue, which made it especially effective. The choice is yours! Intended for indoor use.

4 Draw on any architectural details, such as the roof border, by applying a thick line of craft glue. Cover with sand and shake off. Once you are happy with how your birdhouse looks, allow to dry and set.

5 Gather together your assorted seashells and findings and glue them one by one along the base of the structure. Heavier objects, such as the starfish, may need extra glue and time or the use of a hot glue gun.

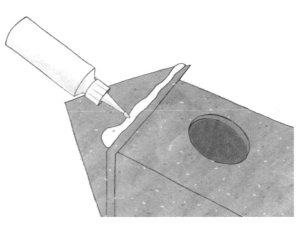

STEP 4

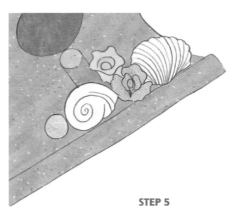

STEP 5

natural wreath

A cache of coastline charms and small romantic notions combine in a relaxed pattern to create an enchanting wreath. Lighten the dark wood of a grapevine wreath to white and aqua, and dot with treasures in a serene palette that takes its cue from frosted sea glass. Hang with fabric to bring littoral loveliness to any locale.

MATERIALS

Grape vine or wicker wreath
Sea glass
Seashells
Starfish
Millinery flowers
Paper roses
Corsage pins (pearl-headed dressmaker's pins)
Fabric

TOOLS

Paint (acrylic craft or spray) in white or aqua
Craft glue
Foam brush
Hot glue gun
Paper plate as palette for paint
Scissors
Wax paper to protect your work surface

1 Grape vine wreaths are naturally quite dark so start this project by applying a few coats of white spray paint, allowing plenty of time to dry between coats. Spray paint will work best for covering the intricate bundles of vines. Suspend the wreath on some dowel or string and ideally paint outside, or in a well-ventilated area.

2 Once the wreath is all white and completely dry, use a dry foam brush to add light strokes of aqua paint to random parts of the wreath.

3 Gather your assorted objects and determine how you will place them on the wreath. Then carefully stick one at a time onto the wreath, using the hot glue gun.

STEP 1

STEP 2

STEP 3

4 Tear a strip of floral fabric and affix a starfish or similar object close to the center. Once this is set, loop the fabric through the wreath for hanging.

5 Finish by attaching millinery flowers with corsage pins (pearl-headed dressmaker's pins): simply push them into the wreath to secure.

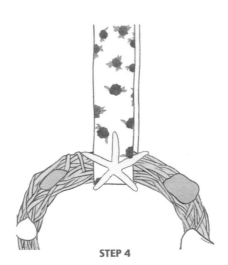

STEP 4

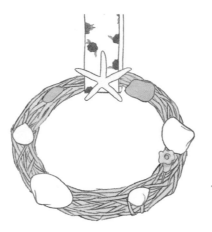

STEP 5

TINKER TIP To save time, suspend the wreath from a dowel and roll it around occasionally, so that you can spray-paint all sides at once.

FANCY THIS The project is suitable for wreaths of any size, from very small to large. Small wreaths can be used to decorate packages or hang from windows or chair backs.

fanciful flip-flops

Festoon everyday flip-flops into frilly footwear that can take you from waterside and beyond. Snips of fastened fabrics add flourish on a shoestring to these vibrant and inexpensive summertime staples.

MATERIALS
Fabric
Pair of flip-flop sandals

TOOLS
Scissors

1 Use a sharp pair of scissors to cut strips of fabric into 1-in (2.5-cm) wide strips that are long enough to tie around the flip-flop straps—about 4–5 in (10–12 cm). Experiment to see what suits your style best.

STEP 1

2 Tie each fabric strip tightly to the Y-shaped strap of the sandal, forming a knot and leaving as little space as possible between each tied strip. As you progress you may need to push the knots closer together. Continue tying until the Y-strap is completely covered.

3 Once you have finished, fluff-up the fabric to see if any spots need adjusting or trimming.

STEP 2

TINKER TIP Cut plenty of pieces of fabric to start with so that when you begin tying, you won't need to stop too many times. Also, use soft, lightweight fabrics that will be comfortable against your skin.

FANCY THIS Coordinate your favorite beach bag to match by giving the handles the same knotty treatment.

STEP 3

chapter 2
tinkering shoreline supplies

Have you ever seen a face in the folds of a blanket, or the shape of a whale in a puffy white cloud? The projects in this chapter encourage you to take notice of the hidden potential in the commonplace. Marvel at how snipped squares can resemble dulled shards of sea glass, white margins on paint cards can stand in as upright masts, and stacks of folded lunch bags can convert into pocketed scrapbooks.

sea-glass mosaic frame

Even several summers of beachcombing can yield very few pieces of precious beach glass. Put down your pail and head to the paint store where you can select paint chip cards in the colors you seek. Pick rectangles of sturdy stock in the coveted hues of frosted tumbled bottles and snip them into jagged shapes for use on a cheerful home accent that will transport you to the seashore.

MATERIALS
Unfinished wood picture frame
Paint color chips cards in muted shades of blue, aqua, green, and lavender

TOOLS
Wax paper to protect your work surface
Foam brush
Paint (acrylic craft, latex or spray) in a pale color
Scissors
Craft glue
Paper plates for palettes
Decoupage medium

FANCY THIS Use this technique to put a summery spin on any flat surface, even furniture (just be sure to seal well for durability). For a romantic spin, photograph and print out your favorite china dish patterns, and snip and use to create shabby-chic style faux mosaic pieces.

1 Remove any glass or plastic insert from the frame prior to painting. Using a dry foam brush, apply a few light coats of white or a pale color paint to create a subtle background. Allow to dry.

2 Using your frame as your guide for sizing, snip the paint chip cards into rectangular shapes that resemble shards of beach glass. Make sure they are not all uniform in shape and size and cut a few of them into triangles. Size them so that you will be able to create two rows with space surrounding each piece.

3 You can either play around with the pieces until you are happy or just dive right in and start gluing. Use craft glue to stick each piece to the frame.

4 Once the frame is decorated to your liking, apply a light coat of decoupage medium over the entire surface using a dry foam brush. Repeat as needed.

STEP 1

STEP 2

STEP 3

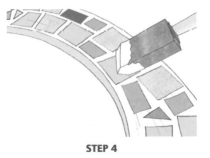

STEP 4

paper lunch bag scrapbook

Fold a stack of paper lunch bags into keepers of memories that are easy to assemble and quick to fill. These small tomes are just right for chronicling day trips or favorite eateries. Creases create pockets and flaps that are perfect for stuffing with ticket stubs and other memorabilia to swap, share, and enjoy.

MATERIALS
Paper lunch bags
Ribbon
Pretty paper (see page 16)
Fabric
Buttons and gems
to embellish

TOOLS
Pencil
Hole punch
Glue stick
Craft glue

1 Note: I used four white paper lunch bags but you could use fewer or more bags and in different colors or sizes. Lay the bags flat on top of each other, alternating the tops and bottoms. Shuffle them into a neat stack and carefully fold in two—smooth out using the barrel of a pen to help sharpen the crease. If the stack is too cumbersome, fold them two at a time.

STEP 1

2 At the folded spine of the bags, punch two holes. You may need to do these one by one so use the top bag as your template and mark where holes will need to be punched with a pencil. Return all bags to a neat stack and weave a ribbon through the top holes down and back through to the bottom holes so that your booklet is bound. Tie the loose ends of the ribbon into a bow. Decide which side will be your back and which your front. I decided to keep the tied ends concealed in the back.

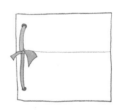

STEP 2

3 Decorate your book by sticking a pretty paper square to the front using glue stick.

STEP 3

4 Cut a small piece of fabric to fit onto the paper square. Mark where it will go and draw a line of craft glue on the paper along three sides (leave the top open so it forms a pocket). Stick the fabric square onto the paper.

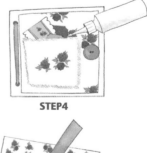

STEP4

5 Open each page and decorate by folding and gluing pieces of pretty paper, fabric, ribbon, stickers, and gems. Fill with small souvenirs and ephemera.

6 Glue short strips of fabric to the front and back edges to tie-shut, if desired, and embellish with a button.

STEP 5

breezy sails mobile

Add jaunty flair to any spot with a fleet of floating sailboats crafted from colorful paint chips. Use the white margins between shades as masts as you snip simple sails to string along lengths of striped baker's twine. Suspend indoors and keep watch as your vessels swirl with each gentle breath of wind.

MATERIALS
Assorted paper paint chip cards from your local paint seller
Baker's twine
Embroidery hoop
Pretty paper (see page 16)

TOOLS
Scissors
Small hole punch
Glue stick
Small foam brush
Decoupage medium (optional)

1 Take a selection of paint chips and decide which colors you want to use. Using the white lines between the colors as a "mast," snip two diagonal lines to a point to form a sail. Use this first sail as a template to cut more. Each sail should be double-sided so trim pairs of matching sails.

2 Trim a hull shape from a solid portion of the paint chip card and use it as a template to cut more—again, making sure you have two matching pieces for each boat. As you snip your sailboats, determine by size just how many you will want to make for your mobile. Consider how long you want each dangling string to be, how many boats per string, and how close together around the hoop base.

3 Once all of your sails and hulls are complete, use a small hole punch to make two holes in the top and bottom of each piece. Thread baker's twine through the holes—depending on the size of the hole and weight of the string, the pieces should stay put; if not, secure with a dab of glue.

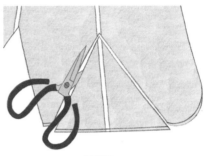

STEP 1

STEP 2

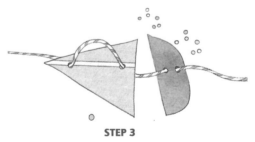

STEP 3

540C-2 ᵁ

4 Cover the inner ring of an embroidery hoop with thin strips of pretty paper, cutting and folding them to fit. Use glue stick to stick them to the ring and then use a small foam brush to brush over the paper with a light coat of decoupage medium, if desired.

5 Cut three long lengths of baker's twine and knot them together close to the top. Tie the other ends of the three pieces to the hoop, spacing them equally apart. Hang the hoop and adjust the strings as needed so that it suspends horizontally and levelly. Tie on the prepared strings of sailboats.

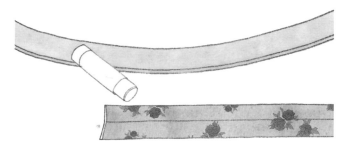

STEP 4

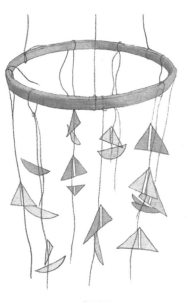

STEP 5

TINKER TIP This project is meant to be displayed indoors.

FANCY THIS Not a boat person? Create kites instead by snipping diamond shapes around the white margins of the paint chips. Attach a small piece of baker's twine with little bows tied on at the bottom of each kite for added flair.

pretty pail

Turn an austere silver pail from a hardware store into a striped seaside charmer by bedecking it with wide strips of rosy-patterned papers. Handy for collecting shells, holding colorful balls of yarn, or as a romantic wine cooler, this splashy and spacious carryall is sure to make all others pale in comparison.

MATERIALS
Silver metal pail
Pretty paper (see page 16)

TOOLS
Scissors
Paper cutter (optional)
Pencil
Glue stick
Wax paper to protect your work surface
Foam brush
Decoupage medium
Blow dryer
Varnish (optional)

1 Begin with an inexpensive silver metal pail; be sure to remove any price stickers. Measure the height of the pail, from just under the rim to the base and make a note of this measurement. Gather an assortment of your favorite papers and cut into wide strips that are the same height as the pail. You may want to use a paper cutter for this task.

2 Before you start to stick on the strips, deal with the most difficult part—cut a hole in two of your strips of paper to accommodate the bases of the handle. You can do this by measuring, estimating, or by pressing a scrap piece of paper against the area to make an impression and then using it as a cutting template.

3 Cover the reverse of each paper strip with glue stick and then apply to the exterior of the bucket, adjusting and smoothing as you go. As an alternative, simply apply torn scraps to make a random collage pattern.

4 Use a foam brush to apply a coat of decoupage medium to seal. Allow to dry and repeat as many times as necessary. If you find the paper bubbling, smooth with your fingers while applying low-directed heat from a blow dryer.

5 If you plan to use your pretty pail outside you will need to repeat the above step with a coat of polyurethane, non-yellowing varnish.

STEP 1

STEP 2

STEP 3

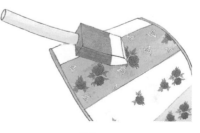

STEP 4

message in a bottle

No longer just for scientific use, small cork-topped bottles are now coveted by savvy crafters. Fill them with glitter, shells, sand, and beads to encapsulate the sparkle of the sea, or tuck in scrolled love notes, invitations, or small fortunes as unexpected tokens of affection. Add a finishing touch with delicate trimmings.

MATERIALS
Corked vials

Fillers such as tiny shells, beads, gems, glitter, sand

Small squares of Pretty paper (see page 16)

Trimming such as lace, seam binding, fabric strips, baker's twine, millinery flowers

TOOLS
Scissors

Toothpick

Paper plate to use as glitter or sand tray

1 For messages, cut a small piece of pretty paper just shorter than the length of the bottle. Write a note on the inside, roll up tightly, and tie with a piece of baker's twine. Use a toothpick to help roll the paper in as small a scroll as possible.

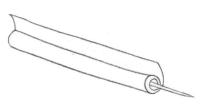

STEP 1

2 For treasures, fill the tube with an assortment of tiny items, such as shells and beads. To give the appearance of sand, add in a pinch of light colored glitter and, once the cork is back on the top, give the bottle a gentle shake. If you are using real sand, make sure it is clean and dry.

STEP 2

3 Wrap your filled vials with short pieces of lace, seam binding, ribbon, or fabric strips. For a final flourish tuck a millinery flower sprig into the top or dot with a gem.

TINKER TIP No sand, no worries. A pinch of table salt or glitter in a pale shade, such as white, gold, or aqua, makes a perfect substitute for a capsule of coastal gems.

FANCY THIS For added whimsy hang a little note from the bottle. Use several bottles to keep small amounts of tiny supplies to hand, such as seed beads. Display a collection of filled tubes in a short glass jar.

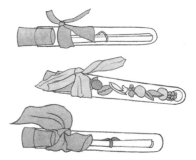

STEP 3

summertime clock

Bring the casual style and thrown-together feel of a summer rental to any space with this unique wall accent, assembled mostly from needlecraft notions. Almost effortless to make, lightweight and ready to hang, you'll always be able to take your sweet time when this clock is on watch.

MATERIALS
Embroidery hoop (you will need both pieces)

Piece of cardboard larger than hoop

Clock movement kit and battery

Fabric

4 large and 8 small Venice lace rosebud appliqués (you can also use flat-bottomed objects, such as buttons, cabochons, or gems)

TOOLS
Pencil

Scissors

Masking tape

Craft glue

TINKER TIP Use the reverse of fabric for an instant sun-faded effect.

FANCY THIS Make multiple fabric clock faces to celebrate special events or to switch out for seasons.

Hang in a group with other embroidery hoops that display needlework and/or pretty fabrics.

1 Begin by loosening the screws of the embroidery hoop to separate it into two sections. With a pencil, trace around the smaller hoop onto a sturdy piece of cardboard. Cut out the cardboard circle.

2 Open the clock movement kit and determine the size hole you will need to create to fit the post (the tube on which the hands attach) through the cardboard. Using the sharp end of a pair of scissors, bore a small hole through the cardboard, which the post can fit through snugly.

3 Place the cardboard circle under your piece of fabric and make a small mark where a hole needs to be cut; snip a small hole in the fabric.

4 Next, place the fabric over the smaller hoop. Frame the smaller hoop within the larger one, adjusting the screws as needed to loosen or tighten. Center and pull the fabric taut enough through the narrow space between the hoops until smooth and then tighten the screws.

STEP 2

STEP 3

STEP 4

5 Back the small fabric covered-hoop using the cardboard circle and, following the instructions for the clock movement kit, assemble so only the post sticks through the cardboard and fabric; complete the clock by attaching the hands and any parts.

6 Trim and/or tuck away any overhanging fabric; use a bit of glue to set. Use pieces of masking tape to stick the cardboard circle to the inside of the hoop to stop it slipping.

7 Lay the clock down (resting on its movement) and glue the four large and eight small flower appliqués in place where numbers would be. Allow to dry and set before hanging on the wall.

STEP 5

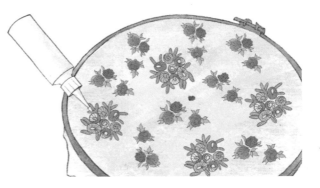

STEP 7

seaside striped coasters

There's something about a striped design that evokes the salty air of the seaside. Add that feel to any setting with coasters made of plank flooring tile, or squares cobbled from craft sticks. Unify with lines of sun-bleached taffy pink over a wash of coarse white paint and use to bring casual style to your coffee table.

MATERIALS

Plank flooring tiles (laminate floor tiles) or squares of plywood
Craft sticks

TOOLS

Pencil, ruler, hacksaw (optional)
Craft glue
Wax paper to protect your work surface
Paper plate for paint palette
Paint (acrylic craft or latex) in white and a second color
Foam brush
Small paintbrush
Decoupage medium

1 Look for plank flooring tiles or plywood in your local home improvement store—the lighter the faux wood finish, the easier it will be to cover with white paint. You may need to cut larger pieces into small squares; if this is the case, use a pencil and ruler to measure accurately (you are looking for a square that is 4 in/10 cm) and cut to size with a hacksaw.

2 Alternatively, you can make your coasters with craft sticks. Neatly line up 12 craft sticks and secure with two sticks glued across the top and bottom, leaving a small margin at the tips. Repeat to make as many coasters as desired.

3 Apply a coat or two of white paint using a dry foam brush. Paint stripes in a second color; you can either do this freehand with a paintbrush or by applying masking tape and using a foam brush to fill in the gaps. Removing the tape before the paint is completely dry will give you slightly uneven lines but, like me, you may like this distressed effect.

4 Use a foam brush to cover both types of squares with several coats of decoupage medium. This will seal the coasters and make them waterproof. Allow each coat to dry between applications.

STEP 1

STEP 3

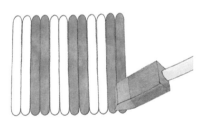

STEP 4

TINKER TIP To create the sun-bleached pink in this project I mixed a dollop of white acrylic craft paint with a bit of a deep pink until it produced the color I wanted. To allow the grain of the wood to show through, apply the paint with a very light hand.

FANCY THIS Once you've mastered the technique of striping on small surfaces, expand your horizons and try your hand at furniture painting. Look for secondhand solid wood furniture; give a quick sanding followed by a good cleaning with something like white vinegar, and then apply a coat of latex paint. Once dry, add stripes using latex or craft paint and then seal the pattern with decoupage medium. For a "distressed" look, rub the corners of the furniture lightly with sandpaper.

pretty pinwheels

Add fanfare to any fête with pleasing pinwheels that gather their unique spin from patterned papers, corsage pins, and striped straws. You can make these in almost any size as long as you begin with a perfect square. Display in tall jars filled with sand or plant into desserts to lend lively panache to any party.

MATERIALS
Paper in coordinating patterns, such as stripes, polka dots, and florals
Paper straws
Corsage pins (pearl-headed dressmaker's pins)

TOOLS
Ruler
Scissors
Glue stick
Small hole punch
Thumb tack (drawing pin)

1 Each pinwheel will require a perfect double-sided square. To do this, you need to either glue two sheets of paper together with their patterned sides exposed and then cut, or cut and then stick them together using a glue stick. Most of the pinwheels shown are made using 4-in (10-cm) squares.

2 Once you have a double-sided square, fold in half and then again so that the square has two intersecting folds, creating four smaller squares. Using scissors, cut a slit from each pointed corner to about ½ in (1 cm) from the center. You will end up with four diagonal slits in the paper, or four "triangles."

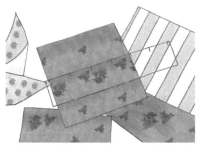

STEP 1

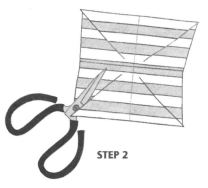

STEP 2

3 Using a small hole punch, make a hole in the left corner of each "triangle" and set aside.

4 Use a thumb tack (drawing pin) to poke a hole into one side of the paper straw, about ½ in (1 cm) from the top.

5 One by one, fold up the holed points of your square and you will see the pinwheel form. Push the corsage (dressmaker's) pin through all four punched holes. Bend the pin at a right angle about ½ in (1 cm) from the top and gently push the pin through the hole in the straw. This ensures that the length of the pin is concealed safely within the tube of the straw, while still allowing the folded fan to spin.

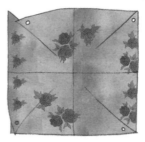

STEP 3

STEP4

STEP 5

TINKER TIP The process of folding the paper into and onto the pin can be awkward. Step 5 shows a sideways view. You may want to practice first on a test paper. You may also want to pre-bend corsage (dressmaker's) pins as needed. You could skip punching small holes into the paper points and simply join by pushing pins through.

FANCY THIS Experiment with using a variety of papers and scales to infuse gatherings with personality and local flavor. Think: old maps and travel brochures, wallpaper scraps and paper gift or shopping parcels.

pleasant dreams catcher

A traditional Ojibwe dreamcatcher is designed to capture the bad dreams while letting the good ones pass and cascade down the trailing feathers to their sleeper. This tinkered version is sure to add texture, interest, and shape to any space by land or sea.

MATERIALS
Cotton fabric
Embroidery hoop (inner or outer hoop)
Feathers

TOOLS
Craft glue
Butterfly clamp (optional)
Scissors

TINKER TIP Add variations such as brightly colored ribbon or beads, gems, or paper roses just above the feathers.

1 Begin by tearing your cotton fabric into narrow strips. You will need long strips for wrapping and shorter strips for dangling (see Tearing paper and fabric, page 19).

2 Gently but tightly wrap the embroidery hoop with fabric strips. Secure at the ends and at intervals with a dab of craft glue—you may want to use a butterfly clamp or similar to hold in place until dry.

3 Once your hoop is covered, secure a long strip of fabric to it, again using glue and clamping until set if needed. Next, begin to wrap the fabric strip over and under the hoop as if you are making a star. You may need to do this a few times until the pattern that gets formed is to your liking; once this is finished, secure any loose ends with glue.

4 To prepare the dangling strands, join the quill of a feather to the end of a fabric strip. Place a dab of glue on the end of the feather and pinch and roll the end of the fabric strip around it. Allow to dry. Do this to as many strips as you like. Tie the loose ends to the base of the hoop.

5 Run a final strip of fabric through a gap at the top of the hoop for hanging in your chosen place.

STEP 2

STEP 3

STEP 4

chapter 3
tinkering rustic recyclables

Add shanty-chic touches throughout your living quarters with appealing and clever accents altered from recycling-bin rescues. Cans, bottles, jars—even plastic grocery bags and cracker boxes—are reused in the most enchanting ways as luminaries, postcards, accessories, and more. Chances are that you already have most of the supplies you need.

cracker box postcards

Make even a weekend at home feel like a carefree get-away by crafting and sending your own postcards. This project makes wonderful use of empty boxes ready for recycling and the smallest scraps of paper. Design quilt-like collages or attach your paper with wild abandon. Recipients of these one-of-a-kind greetings are sure to wish they were there, too.

MATERIALS
Cardboard packaging from cracker and cookie boxes
Pretty paper (see page 16)

TOOLS
Scissors
Paper cutter (optional)
Glue stick
Decoupage medium
Foam brush

1 To ensure that your postcard arrives at its destination, be sure to follow a few guidelines: postcards must be rectangular in shape, at least 3½ x 5 in (9 x 12 cm) and no more than 4¼ x 6 in (11 x 15 cm). For the examples shown, I simply used a purchased postcard as my template.

2 Flatten your cardboard packaging and first create a cutting template or use a purchased postcard. Trace the shape on the printed side of the cardboard and cut using scissors or a paper cutter.

3 Using a glue stick, decorate the printed side of the card with a collage of pretty paper, and leave the plain brown underside for messages and for the address.

4 Be sure that the paper collages on the postcard are nice and flat. Use decoupage medium lightly to help smooth any loose corners.

STEP 2

STEP 3

STEP 4

tin can luminary

Empty tin cans become sturdy lanterns ready to add glittering light to any dim place that could benefit from a bit of magic. Make as many as you like and use them to cast a subtle glow along a walkway or down some steps, or to add ambiance to a romantic dinner served outside on a warm summer night.

MATERIALS
Tin can

TOOLS
Small hammer
Nails, width and size depending on your preference
Paint (metal, latex, or spray)
Paper plate as paint palette
Foam brush
Wire for hanging

TINKER TIPS To loosen a stubborn label, submerge the can in warm, soapy water and leave overnight.

Work quickly to make all the holes before the ice melts, but take care when hammering and focus on completing one hole at a time.

Take all the usual precautions when using candles, or use small battery-operated votives.

The handle from a Chinese food take-out carton makes a good hanging device.

FANCY THIS Hammer out other patterns such as numbers, simple flower shapes, and stars.

1 Prepare the cans by removing any labels and washing and drying the cans thoroughly inside and out to avoid rusting. Carefully tap down any jagged edges with a small hammer.

2 Fill the can almost to the top with water and place in the freezer for a couple of hours—you need the water inside to just-freeze. Leaving the can in the freezer for an extended period of time can cause the bottom to expand and warp, making it unsteady as a fixture.

3 Remove the can from the freezer and draw a simple shape such as a heart on the best side of the can.

4 Prepare a sturdy surface where you can hammer a pattern into the can. The best bets are a table over a cork board or cutting board, or outdoors at a picnic table, with the can supported by a couple of bricks propped on a dishtowel. Carefully hammer the end of a nail just through the can and then pull out; repeat at intervals around the shape to create a pattern of small holes. If you plan to hang your luminary, make two holes at the top of the can on either side so you can attach a handle. When all the hammering is completed, drain and dry the can.

5 Use a foam brush to paint the can using a craft paint meant for metal, or latex paint. You can also use spray paint but be prepared for occasional drips. Apply as many coats as desired, allowing the can to dry thoroughly between coats.

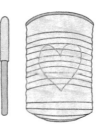

STEP 3

STEP 4

STEP 6

6 If you want to hang your luminary, thread a sturdy piece of wire through and fasten well either by bending or tying.

twined tidies

Brighten and organize any room by spinning simple tin cans into shanty-chic caddies. Wrap cans in baker's twine using a plethora of summery shades, from sunset to citrus to salt water taffy, and further embellish with ribbon and rosebuds. Make and group tidies in related shades to keep supplies cheerfully within reach.

MATERIALS
Tin cans
Striped baker's twine
Short length of seam binding or ribbon
Rosebud appliqué or other embellishment

TOOLS
Small hammer
Paint (metal, latex, or spray)
Paintbrush (optional)
Craft glue

TINKER TIP To help wrap the cans evenly, set up a small barrier, such as a book, to hold the spool in place so that as you pull the twine it stays taut.

FANCY THIS Use this technique to add texture and color to other barrel-shaped objects, such as bottles and jars.

1 Prepare the cans by removing labels and washing them thoroughly. Allow the cans to dry completely both inside and out to avoid any rusting later, which would spoil your work. Carefully tap down any jagged edges at the open top of the can with a small hammer.

2 Paint the can using a craft paint meant for metal, latex paint, or spray paint. Apply as many coats of paint as desired, allowing the can to dry thoroughly between each coat. Painting the bottom and inside of the can is also optional.

3 Dab a bit of glue onto a small section of the can and, starting from either the top or the bottom, carefully wrap the twine around, holding the glued end in place with your thumb to secure. Keep wrapping the twine tightly around the can—occasionally you might need to push the forming bands closer together and even unwrap and re-wrap a bit until the pattern suits you.

4 When you reach the other end of the can, trim the twine and secure the end with a dab of glue. You can conceal the glue by rubbing it gently in the direction of the twine.

5 Measure around the can and cut a length of seam binding or ribbon to fit; secure with craft glue. Add another dab of glue and stick on a rosebud appliqué or other embellishment.

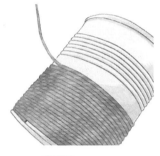

STEP 3

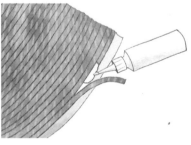

STEP 4

STEP 5

ship in a jar

In this no-strings-attached approach to the old maritime craft of making a ship in a bottle, boats are mounted upright in wide-mouthed jars amid a sparkling sea of shimmering baubles. Enjoy building and assembling a small fleet, and impress your friends with your re-imagined regatta.

MATERIALS
Toothpick
Small craft sticks
Wide-mouthed jar with lid
Pretty paper (see page 16)
Beads

TOOLS
Wax paper to protect your
work surface
Craft glue or hot glue gun
Paper plate as palette
for paint
Paint (acrylic craft, latex,
or spray)
Foam brush or small
paintbrush
Scissors
Glue stick
Decoupage medium

1 Build a small boat by breaking off one sharp end of a toothpick. Use craft glue or a hot glue gun to attach the flat end upright to the center of a small craft stick to create a mast. Allow the glue to set and then apply a coat of paint to the entire boat. Repeat to make a small fleet.

2 For each sail take a square of pretty paper, about 3 x 3 in (8 x 8 cm). Fold in half diagonally and then cut along the crease to create two triangles. Apply glue stick to the reverse of one triangle and then stick the two triangles together with the toothpick sandwiched in between. You should now have a tiny sailboat. Put a dab of glue at the bottom of the "boat" and stick firmly inside a jar that is lying on its side.

3 Decorate the lid of the jar by cutting a circle and band of pretty paper to fit. Stick using glue stick and seal with a coat of decoupage medium.

4 Once the boat has dried and set inside the jar, add just enough beads to cover the hull and return the lid to the jar.

STEP 1

STEP 2

STEP 3

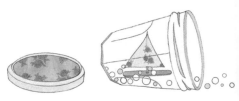

STEP4

FANCY THIS These little sailboats are equally adorable on their own, berthed along a shelf.

bubbly soda bottles and caddy

Beach house dining at its most relaxed can mean eating around the sofa, picnic table, or even fire pit. Skip the formality but add some frippery by prettying up pop bottles. Makeover a six-pack using doilies, floral papers, and delicate trimmings. Refill empty bottles with either sparkling drinks or tall, fresh flowers for an effervescent and inventive table setting.

MATERIALS
Six-pack of soda bottles in cardboard caddy
Pretty paper (see page 16), including cardstock and labels or decorative tape
Doilies
Trimming, such as ribbon or pompom

TOOLS
Craft glue
Decorative paper punch
Glue stick
Paper plate as palette
Decoupage medium
Pattern-edged scissors
Ruler
Scissors
Clothespins
Wax paper to protect your work surface

1 If using empty bottles, prepare them by removing labels and washing and drying thoroughly inside. If using full bottles, decorate them while at room temperature.

2 Gather an assortment of supplies: full sheets of pretty paper and cardstock, paper doilies, trimming, and decorative punches. Measure areas that you want to cover with pieces of paper, such as the tall neck of the bottle or the wide body. Cut and trim shapes to fit, apply glue stick to the reverse, and press on gently. Smooth out any wrinkles and wipe away any glue smears to avoid cloudiness on the glass.

3 To cover your caddy, take a few sheets of pretty paper and use a pencil, ruler, and scissors to cut pieces to fit. Stick to the caddy using glue stick, smoothing down any creases and turning about 1 in (2.5 cm) over the edges to neaten. Use clothespins to hold the paper securely until it sets firm, and hide any paper seams by adding doilies as finishing touches.

4 Finish by adding embellishments, such as decorative pompom trim, to the bottle necks.

STEP 2

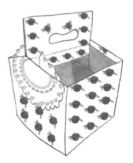

STEP 3

STEP 4

TINKER TIP Use sturdy paper, such as fabric copied onto cardstock or heavier scrapbooking paper, for covering the caddy so that it stays strong. You may need to use craft glue instead of glue stick to attach heavier paper.

FANCY THIS Create a stunning showcase by filling dry bottles with layers of tinted salt (see Hurricane Candle Holder, page 124).

FANCY THIS If using objects collected on far-away travels, add a label to the jar to say where they come from, or create a small sign to go inside the vignette including the name of the place.

tinkered terrariums

Bring bits of the shoreline to any spot with charming waterside vignettes set over sand. Use notions and natural objects to compose idyllic scenes. Showcase miniature dioramas in colorfully topped canning jars and festoon with tiny bunting made from fabric scraps. Unlike typical terrariums this version requires no upkeep; just play and display.

MATERIALS

Toothpicks or wood craft picks
(slightly wider)
Baker's twine
Fabric scraps
Pretty paper (see page 16)
Assorted natural objects, such
as lavender buds, small
seashells, pebbles
Embellishments, such as
cabochons, cupcake toppers,
gems, paper roses
Canning jar with two-piece
metal lid (flat lid
and screw-on band)
Cupcake liner
Sand

TOOLS

Scissors
Craft glue
Paint (metal or latex)
Foam brush
Tweezers
Wax paper to protect
work surface

1 First think about the scene you would like to make. I love images of floral linen tents so I fashioned a sort of teepee by joining three toothpicks with some baker's twine and covered them with a rectangular scrap of fabric.

2 Make deckchairs to match by folding scraps of paper and gluing them to pebble bases.

3 Another idea is to build a small picket fence from wooden craft picks. Give it a light wash of white paint and glue on a few paper roses.

4 Once you have made the scene for your terrarium, prepare your jar for filling. Make sure your jar and lid are completely clean and dry. Paint the screw-on band of the lid using latex paint or craft paint meant for metal. Let dry completely.

5 Fill the jar with sand—about 1 in (2.5 cm) should be enough. If you don't have sand, use tinted salt (see the Hurricane Candle Holder, page 124), or even turbinado or demerara sugar. Carefully place your items into the sand—you may find tweezers easier for this. Scatter in small shells, beads, and lavender buds, if you wish.

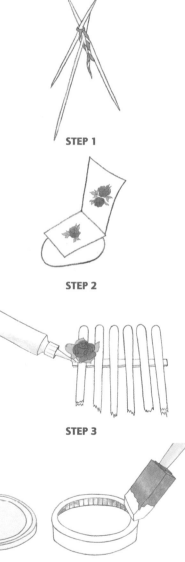

STEP 1

STEP 2

STEP 3

STEP4

6 Separate the canning jar lid into its two sections. Flatten a cupcake liner, center it over the flat part, and frame by returning the ring section.

7 Decorate the outside of the jar by making small bunting using either fabric or paper scraps. Either snip triangles and glue directly onto baker's twine or trim triangles at folded creases to create diamond shapes to fold over and glue to the twine.

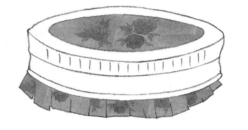

STEP 6

STEP 7

grocery bag bunting and sandcastle flags

Transform any mound of sand into a castle and any outdoor space into a carnival with flags and bunting made from grocery bags. Chances are you already have a vibrant collection of colored bags in a cupboard or hanging behind a door. Reusable and recyclable, solid or patterned, if they're plastic or vinyl, they're waterproof, so cut them up and bedeck your outside spaces!

MATERIALS
Colorful plastic grocery bags and/or oilcloth
Baker's twine
Toothpicks or wood craft picks

TOOLS
Scissors
Craft glue
Butterfly clamps or clips
Construction paper for template
Clothespins (optional)

1 Start by creating a template from a sturdy piece of paper. Fold it in half and crease well. Mark and cut a triangle shape with the fold as the bottom edge, so that when opened you should have a diamond shape to use as your template. Make a small diamond template for the sandcastle flags and a larger diamond template for the bunting (approximately 4 in/10 cm high).

2 Cut the sides of your plastic grocery bags to open them up and create larger pieces. Fold sections in half and crease well or use existing creases. Slip your template over the crease and trace with a pencil. Then cut out.

STEP 1

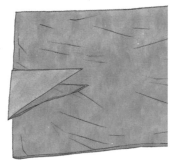

STEP 2

3 For the bunting, cut as many diamonds as needed, lay them out flat and open and apply craft glue to the wrong side, making sure to cover the edges. Lay baker's twine along the inner crease and close the diamond along the string, making sure the edges are lined up. You may need to hold pieces closed until the glue has set, either by weighting down with something heavy or securing with clothespins.

4 For sandcastle flags, lay the small diamonds flat and apply glue as before. Slip a toothpick into the fold, positioning it toward the top. Close the diamond along the toothpick, press to smooth as needed, and allow to dry.

STEP 3

STEP 4

TINKER TIPS

Keep a supply of sandcastle flags in your beach bag so that you are always ready to festoon a fortress.

The sharper your scissors, the easier it will be to cut up plastic grocery bags.

FANCY THIS Make extra flags to pitch in sandwiches and turn a picnic into a party.

water flowers

As a little girl I was fascinated by taped-shut seashells for sale in souvenir stores. When placed in water, the tape would disintegrate and tall blossoms would emerge from the shells. In this tinkered version, flowers are fashioned from plastic and anchored to decorated stones and shells in water. Assemble for an unexpected display brimming with nostalgia.

MATERIALS

Stones and shells
Pretty paper (see page 16) or paper flower motifs
Grocery bags made from thin plastic
Baker's twine or other lightweight thread
Vase

TOOLS

Scissors
Glue stick
Decoupage medium
Foam brush
Paper plate as palette
Small hole punch
Tape (invisible or decorative)

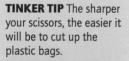

TINKER TIP The sharper your scissors, the easier it will be to cut up the plastic bags.

FANCY THIS Make the project on a much smaller scale to display in small jars and juice glasses.

1 Decorate your stones and shells with tiny floral motifs—either cut them from pretty paper or use paper motifs. Affix to the stone or shell using the glue stick and then apply several coats of decoupage medium to waterproof them. You could seal them even further with a coat of varnish or clear nail polish.

2 To create your flowers, take a grocery bag made of very thin, recyclable plastic—ideally white or in a pale color. Cut several small squares, approximately 2 x 2 in (5 x 5 cm). Position 3–5 of them in a stack—this will make one flower. Lightly draw a simple flower shape onto the stack of squares and cut out.

3 Using a small hole punch, make two holes close to each other in the center of each flower (like on a button) and weave a long piece of baker's twine through. Tie it into a tight knot to secure the layers. Cut a few short snips around the plastic; this will later help to form petals.

4 Circle the flower over one hand and pull the twine down through using your other hand, causing the plastic to push up into a flower shape. Pinch together the base that has formed and secure with a piece of tape. Fluff up the petals until the flower looks right.

5 Tie each flower to a decorated stone or shell and gently place into a voluminous vase or jar. Carefully fill with water and display.

STEP 1

STEP 2

STEP 3

STEP 4

reverse canvas frame

The understated beauty of solid wood and stapled cotton provide the perfect backdrop for favorite photographs and collected ocean gems. With the flip of an art canvas and tacked twine for hanging, you'll have a frame with a narrow perch just right for staging a tableau. Rig to hang vertically or horizontally. Display one or make many to turn a galley into a gallery.

MATERIALS

Art canvas in wooden frame

Photographs, postcards, images from brochures, or travel catalogs

Assorted objects such as seashells, small sea star, sea glass

Pretty paper (see page 16)

Glitter

Twine or string

TOOLS

Ruler

Scissors

Glue stick

Craft glue

Glue pen

Toothpick (optional)

Paper plate for glitter tray

Thumb tacks (drawing pins)

Wax paper to protect your work surface

1 Look through photographs, postcards, and travel brochures to find an image you think will work best in your frame. Gather objects to display in your frame, such as seashells, pebbles, or pieces of glass. Measure and cut a piece of plain or patterned paper to fill the inside of the back of the frame and secure it with glue stick.

2 If you want to add glitter to the main image, draw fine lines to selected areas using either a glue pen or a toothpick dipped in craft glue. Apply the glitter, one color at a time, and shake off the excess.

3 Determine where you will position the main image and affix using glue stick. Experiment with placing different objects on the bottom shelf of the frame; once you find the look you like, secure in place using craft glue. Allow to dry and set.

4 To prepare your frame for hanging, cut a length of string or twine to the desired length, tie at the ends and secure to the front of the canvas with thumb tacks (drawing pins).

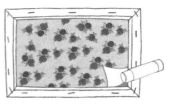

STEP 1

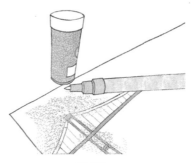

STEP 2

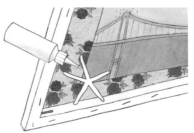

STEP 3

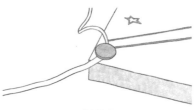

STEP 4

TINKER TIP Add a touch of color by carefully painting the exposed wood on the frame.

FANCY THIS Back with a collage of maps and local menus, or leave the canvas as is for an especially lovely accent in an all-white and natural décor scheme.

chapter 4
tinkering sunny sundries

Create coastal-inspired accents that belie their humble land-locked origins
in this section, which calls for supplies from the pantry as well as the craft
store. Piece together patterns with pasta, tint salt into the hues of a hot
summer sunset, construct a pint-sized beach haven from craft sticks,
and more. Enjoy making these projects with the same ease and serenity
of a childhood art lesson.

tinkerer's valentine

Long ago, sailors far from home would piece together intricately patterned gifts of shells from their travels to present to their sweethearts. Usually heart-shaped, they became known as sailor's valentines. This version doesn't require a voyage, much time, or even many real shells, but can be just as sentimental.

MATERIALS

Heart-shaped wooden box
Fabric
1 white paper rose
5 small shells, such as ribbed cockle shells
Small shell pasta shapes

TOOLS

Pencil
Scissors
Paint (acrylic craft or latex) in your chosen color and white
Paper plate for palette
Small foam brush
Glue stick
Craft glue
Paintbrush

TINKER TIP If you are not confident about painting items already glued onto a surface, you can paint them before adding them on.

FANCY THIS Think outside the heart-shaped box and embellish other flat surfaces. Build designs on pretty paper to frame, or display in a shadow box.

1 Trace around the base of the box onto your chosen fabric and cut out the shape. Repeat for the lid. Cut out both pieces and set aside—you will use these to line the box and lid later.

2 Pour a small amount of paint onto your palette (use a white paper plate or some wax paper) and lighten as desired by mixing in small amounts of white paint and blending. Separate the box from the lid. Using a dry foam brush, give both the box and the lid a few light coats of paint and let dry.

3 When the box and lid are completely dry, affix the fabric hearts onto the base of the box and inside the lid using a glue stick.

4 Glue a white paper rose to the center of the top of the lid and encircle with the five small shells, forming a daisy-like shape. Fill in the five small gaps with small shell pasta shapes. Allow to set.

5 Outline the top of the lid with a border of small shell pasta; place and glue each piece on a slight diagonal to create a roping effect. Allow to dry and set.

6 Using a small, dry paintbrush, carefully paint the shell pasta white. Give a light coat of white paint to the shells and paper flower to unify the decorative elements.

STEP 2

STEP 4

STEP 5

STEP 6

craft stick cottage

Pay homage to the sweet charm of beach cottages with a diminutive property built to suit from popsicle (lolly) sticks. Add drive-by appeal to your inland retreat with playful details that include pastel-hued stripes, window boxes bursting with blooms, and a short section of picket fence. Even in the winter, this shack is sure to keep the cockles of your heart warm.

YOU WILL NEED TO BUILD SIX PANELS: two for the roof and four for the sides. Note that amounts of sticks used may vary due to last-minute adjustments, such as covering any problematic areas. For best results, use craft glue to make panels and doors but use a hot glue gun to assemble all the panels together and for adding details. You will be able to make quick adjustments, such as joining and fitting the roof and adding flower boxes, before the hot glue hardens.

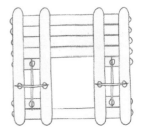

MATERIALS
Box of unfinished craft sticks, in assorted sizes
Wooden toothpicks
Bead or gem
Millinery or paper flowers
Fabric

TOOLS
Wax paper to protect your work surface
Craft glue
Hot glue gun
Scissors
White spray paint
Paintbrush
Paint (acrylic craft or latex) in pastel colors

1 To create a roof panel, lay some longer craft sticks side by side until the width of your roof is the same as the length of one craft stick. Use craft glue to glue two sticks, top and bottom, across the panel to hold the sticks together. Make two of these panels.

STEP 1

2 To build a basic frame for the remaining panels, start by assembling a perfect square from four sticks and secure where each tip meets with dots of glue. Start to fill in the basic frame, using small sticks, trimmed sticks, and toothpicks to fashion windows and doors as desired. The door is made by placing four sticks side by side and gluing a fifth stick on the diagonal to secure.

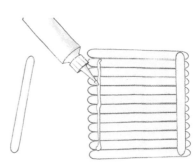

STEP 2

3 Create a window box by gluing two sticks into a bench-like shape and then attaching to the house.

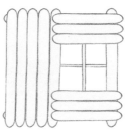

STEP 3

---

4 To make a fence, lay two sticks parallel and place small craft sticks vertically at small intervals to connect.

5 Once you are happy with the panels, it's time to glue the four walls together using the hot glue gun. You may want to use a prop, such as a heavy can, to help position the panels as you glue. Next, glue the two roof panels together at the tips where they meetand then position and glue them onto the house.

6 Add supports by attaching small craft sticks to connect the house to the roof. Glue on any additional structural pieces, such as the door or any window boxes. Attach a short fence to the house by gluing it to a craft stick that has been cut in half. Make any adjustments so that your cottage stands without too much wobble.

7 Paint the entire exterior using spray paint. Once dry, add color to the door, shutters, and roof using craft paint and a small brush.

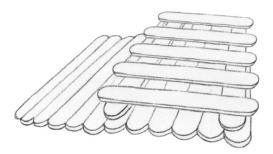

STEP 4

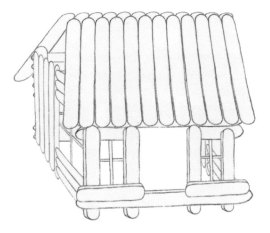

STEP 5

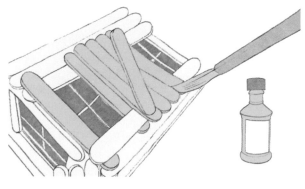

STEP 7

TINKER TIPS Place small seashells or miniature starfish on windows. For best results, keep finished project indoors.

FANCY THIS Place a battery-operated votive inside to illuminate your little cottage at night.

8 Add curb appeal by gluing on a gem for a doorknob and an appliqué wreath, tucking millinery flowers into boxes and gaps, and hanging small squares of fabric (from the inside) for curtains.

STEP 8

merpegs

Craft a seaworthy tale by transforming simple wooden clothespins into mythical maidens offering pearls of wisdom from the deep. All it takes is a few twists of shimmering foil, shiny sequins, and cascades of colorful floss to conjure up these enchanting creatures of legend.

MATERIALS

One-piece wooden clothespin or "doll pin" with round top
Foil candy (petit four) liners
Embroidery floss (thread) for hair
Sequins, faux pearls
Chenille sticks (pipe cleaners)
Foil garland trimming

TOOLS

Clear nail polish
Fine point permanent markers
Scissors
Craft glue

TINKER TIP Substitute foil-lined wrappers with aluminum foil or any pliable paper that can hold a shape, such as the patterned type used for origami.

FANCY THIS Skip the tails and push your Merpegs into cupcakes frosted in waves of sparkling blue to create a magical maritime party theme.

1 Apply a light coat of clear nail polish to the head of the clothespin. This will prevent the ink from bleeding into the wood grain when you draw the face. Allow to dry.

2 Practice how you will draw a face on paper first—I find the simpler, the better. When ready, draw the facial features using permanent markers.

3 Open out a foil liner and remove the paper lining. Flatten the cup into a circle and lay your clothespin on top so that the foil comes just above where the wood separates in two. Roll the pin in the foil and then bend the hollow section of foil upward into a fin shape.

4 Trim two diagonal slits and cut away a small triangle of foil so that the single fin shape becomes two. Pinch the pointed ends into more of a fishtail shape. If you want your merpeg to stand upright, shape the foil at the pin's base until the figure can stand. To secure the foil to the pin, pull it down slightly, add a dot of glue and then return the foil to its position. Press into place and allow to set.

STEP 1

STEP 3

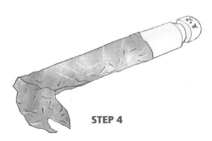

STEP 4

5 To make hair, cut at least 12 strands of embroidery floss about 6 in (15 cm) long. For added whimsy, use pastel colored floss with a few contrasting pieces. Bundle and tie together using one strand; the knot will be where the hair parts. Either leave as it is or pull a few strands from each side together and trim as bangs (fringe). Glue to the top of the pin and let dry.

6 Glue two sequins close to the top of the pin "body" and allow to dry and set.

7 Cut a section of chenille stick approximately 6 in (15 cm) long and bend in half; bend a bit at each end to make little hands and to secure any sharp wire edges. Place the chenille stick behind the neck area of the doll pin; bend and shape until secure around the doll as arms. Glue an offering into the hands, such as a shell, faux pearl, or mini starfish.

8 Cut a small section of foil garland trimming and form into a crown; stick to the merpeg's head with a small dot of glue.

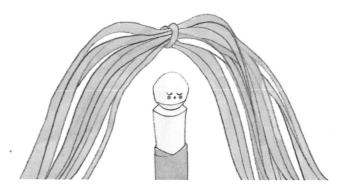

STEP 5

STEP 6

STEP 7

front porch picnic

Add a bit of frivolity in unexpected places with this nod to café society. Fashioned from wooden craft sticks, this pocket-sized furniture can be used to line a sunny windowsill, add lightness to a serious bookcase, or provide perches for favorite collections.

MATERIALS
Long craft sticks (2 per chair)
Small craft sticks
(11 per chair)
Wooden spool
Fabric
Pretty paper (see page 16)
Mini terra-cotta pot
Ribbon
Mini wired paper roses

TOOLS
Craft glue
Hot glue gun (optional)
Paint or spray paint
Scissors

FANCY THIS Create many chairs or sets and paint in varying shades of the same color to display in a row for an ombre effect. Use chairs as a place to stand small items, such as salt and pepper shakers, placecards, or mini cupcakes.

1 Start by making the chairs. For the chair back, lay two craft sticks parallel to each other and attach by gluing two smaller craft sticks across toward one end, leaving a small gap in between. For the seat, lay out five small craft sticks with small gaps between and secure by gluing two small craft sticks across at each end. For the chair legs, cross two sets of small craft sticks with dots of glue at their centers. Allow the four constructed pieces to dry and set well.

2 Glue each set of legs to the bottom of the chair seat where the two craft sticks cross the five sticks. For best results, use something to hold the legs in place while they dry—alternatively use a hot glue gun.

3 Once the pieces have set, position the seat on its side on top of the chair back and glue where wood meets wood. Repeat steps 1 and 2 to make as many chairs as desired.

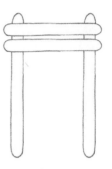

STEP 1

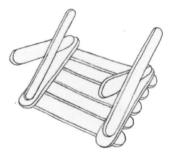

STEP 2

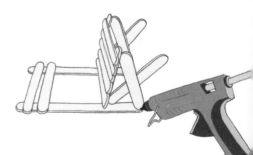

STEP 3

4 To create a table, line six small craft sticks and connect by gluing two small crafts sticks across toward the top and bottom. Use craft glue to stick the wooden spool to the base of the table.

5 Unify the table and chairs into a set by painting them the same color. The project shown was first spray-painted with white primer and then given a coat of acrylic craft paint in pink.

6 Glue a small square of fabric to the table top to serve as a table cloth and wrap the spool with a piece of pretty paper.

7 Spray-paint a small terra-cotta planter using white spray paint. When it is dry, tie a piece of ribbon around it and fill it with faux flowers. Dot each chair with a dot of craft glue and add a small embellishment, such as a paper rose, gem, or cabochon.

STEP 4

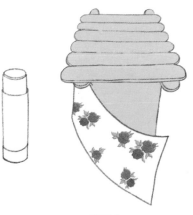

STEP 6

STEP 7

swoonable spoons and cups

Set a stylish dessert buffet with disposable spoons swathed in a lively mix of paper scraps. Display them in a cup, or bundle with napkins and tie with ribbons for portable events. Whether sharing a romantic sundae for two or serving up treats for a crew, this small touch is sure to please every palate.

MATERIALS

Wooden spoons,
6½ in (16 cm) long
Mini wooden dessert spoons,
3¾ in (9.5 cm) long
Pretty paper (see page 16)

TOOLS

Scissors
Construction paper
Glue stick
Decoupage medium (optional)
Foam brush (optional)

1 The sections of the spoons that will come into contact with food should be kept free from paper or glue. Also note that spoons are intended for single use or decorative purposes. Depending on the length of your spoon, you will be measuring and trimming a scrap of paper to fit the handle.

2 For longer spoons, aim for paper to wrap tightly all around the handle once, or trim to fit using different papers on each side. Create a template using colored construction paper once you have determined your measurements. Apply glue stick to the reverse of the paper, place, glue, trim, and smooth as needed.

3 For shorter spoons, it will be easier to create a template first by tracing the handle and then cutting out two pieces per spoon from pretty paper. Stick them to both sides of the spoon with glue stick.

4 Leave the spoons as they are or seal the paper-covered handles with a light coat of decoupage medium. Make sure you avoid the end of the food meant for food handling.

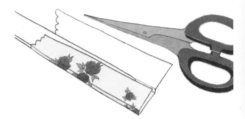

STEP 1

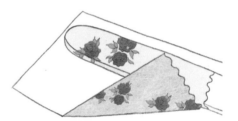

STEP 2

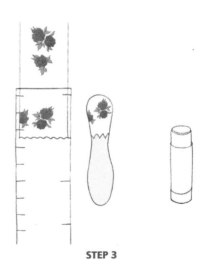

STEP 3

TINKER TIP Trim paper with pattern-edged scissors for added panache.

FANCY THIS Create a scrumptious party set by also covering short paper dessert cups and cones. Simply flatten one to serve as your template and trace, trim, and adhere to a plain cup or cone.

Purchase do-it-yourself plastic insert cups and pots alongside children's crafts but instead of coloring on the paper insert, use it as a template and cut and insert pretty paper.

petite treasure boxes

Add cottage charm to your gift giving with small boxes built from craft sticks. A coat of white paint lends picket fence appeal to these sturdy little parcels that are ready to fill with small prizes and charms. As easy to put together as they are endearing, make extra to use as table decorations or favors.

MATERIALS
Mini craft sticks
Fabric scraps or ribbon
Millinery flowers or
embellishments

TOOLS
Craft glue
Foam brush
Paint (acrylic craft, latex,
or spray)
Wax paper to protect your
work surface

1 Neatly line six mini craft sticks side by side. Secure these with two sticks glued lengthwise across the top and bottom, leaving a small margin at the tips. Set aside as your lid.

2 Repeat step 1 to create the base of your box and continue to build walls up as you would a log cabin, alternating between sides, using dots of craft glue to secure. Continue until the walls are the desired height. Once your box is complete, set aside to dry.

3 For even coverage, use spray paint; for a weathered appearance, apply paint using a dry foam brush. Be sure to paint each side of the box and lid. Apply as many coats as desired and allow to dry completely.

4 Take a narrow strip of fabric to tie around the box. You can either wrap the whole box, as you would a gift, or simply tie the fabric around the lid. Tuck in a sprig of millinery flowers or any appealing embellishment.

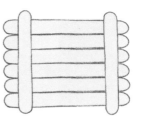

STEP 1

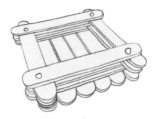

STEP 2

STEP 3

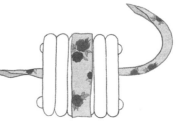

STEP 4

TINKER TIP Remember that the less glue used, the shorter the dry time. Only small dots and thin lines of glue are needed.

FANCY THIS These are just as sweet if you skip tying the lids with fabric and, instead of flowers, top them with seashells.

hurricane candle holder

Ordinary table salt easily changes color when blended with the dust of colored chalk in gentle swirls. Repeat to create a series of colorful dunes and then layer into a wide-mouthed jar. Leave room to plant a votive candle to complete this project, which brings to mind a breezy beach sunset.

MATERIALS

Salt (and Epsom salts for texture variation)
Colored chalk
Wide-mouthed jar, label removed, washed and dried or glass hurricane lamp
Votive candle
Fabric strips

TOOLS

Paper plates as mixing trays
Skewer, plastic knife, or toothpick

1 Pour a small pile of salt onto a paper plate. Select your first chalk color and press down and swirl the chalk around the salt until the salt takes on the color of the chalk. Continue until the desired hue is reached. Set the colored salt aside and repeat to create another color, using a new paper plate for each color. Continue until you have at least three piles of colored salt.

2 Start filling your jar or glass lamp with colored salt, alternating light and dark colors for impact, for example, pink to yellow to blue. Use the paper plate as a funnel to tip the salt into the jar and tilt the jar between colors to create a slanted pattern. Make sure to leave enough empty height for a candle. To create patterns or swirls through the layers use a skewer, plastic knife, or toothpick and poke down from the top along the inside of the jar.

3 Plant the bottom of a candle into the salt so that it is secure.

4 Finish by tying the outside of the jar or lamp with a scrap of fabric.

STEP 1

STEP 2

STEP 3

STEP 4

TINKER TIP Add to the display with non-flammable items, such as small shells, sea glass, or pearl findings.

FANCY THIS Skip the candle and create a coastline of jars along a windowsill; fill the containers and top with lids tinkered to suit.

Suppliers

Annette Tatum
Online retailer
AnnetteTatum.com
Tel: (+1) 888 655 1359
Fabric

Cath Kidston
Online retailer (USA) and stores (UK)
www.CathkidstonUSA.com
www.cathkidston.co.uk
Fabrics

Creating Vintage Charm In-House Designs
Online retailer
www.creatingvintagecharm.com
Designer paper for arts and crafts

Foster's Discount Store
210 New St E, Glassboro, NJ 08028
Millinery flowers, ribbon

Hobbycraft
Stores nationwide UK
www.hobbycraft.com
Arts and craft suppliers

Home Depot
Stores nationwide USA
www.HomeDepot.com
Latex paint, metal pail, plank flooring tile (Stratford Oak 63535), paint chips, spray paint

Ikea
Stores worldwide
www.Ikea.com
Scissors, construction paper, paper napkins

John Lewis
Stores nationwide UK and online retailer
www.johnlewis.com
Fabrics, stationery, kitchen supplies

Kreatelier
Online retailer
Kreatelier.com
Tel: (+1) 401 432 7995
Fabric

Little Pink Studio
Online retailer
www.TheLittlePinkStudio.com
Vintage seam binding, Venice lace rosebud appliqués

MarthaStewart.com
Online retailer
www.MarthaStewart.com
Fine tip glue pen, cupcake liners, adhesive gems, craft paint

Michaels
Stores nationwide USA
www.Michaels.com
Craft tools: glue, decoupage medium, foam brushes, chenille sticks (pipe cleaners), unfinished wood items (birdhouse, frame, doll pegs and stands, spools, craft sticks), cupcake liners, adhesive gems and paper roses, embroidery floss (thread), feathers.

Shabby Fabrics
Online retailer
www.Shabbyfabrics.com
Wide range of pretty fabrics, including Lecien, available to view by color preference

Speckled Egg
Online retailer
www.Speckled-Egg.com
Vintage painted flower cabochons, vintage tiny flower beads

Staples
Stores nationwide USA and UK
www.staples.com
Color copies, paper cutter, mailing labels, Sharpie pens

Sugar Pink Boutique
Online retailer
www.sugarpinkboutique.com
Millinery flowers, fat quarter bundles of fabric, seam binding

The Shoppe At Somerset
Online retailer
www.stampington.com/shoppe
Baker's twine, decorated tape

TJ Maxx
Stores nationwide USA
www.TJMaxx.com
Scrapbooking supplies

TK Maxx
Stores nationwide UK
www.TKMaxx.com
Scrapbooking supplies

Vintage Lizzie
Online retailer
www.vintagelizziestyle.blogspot.com
www.urbangardenstextiles.com
Fabrics featuring antique French roses

Index

Acknowledgments

I feel so incredibly lucky for the opportunity to have spent many blissful hours interpreting my adoration of the seashore and simple crafting into makes and words for my second book. Living in Rhode Island, USA means shipping projects and text in batches to London and trusting the team at CICO Books to work their glorious magic and they always do, beyond my wildest expectations.

Many heartfelt thanks to Cindy Richards for loving the idea for this book from the start and for her ongoing support. Warmest appreciation to Penny Craig, Clare Sayer, and Sally Powell for making sure things made sense, and to Mark McGinlay for his tireless media work and enthusiasm. Thanks also to Lauren Walsh and Kristin Meenagh for their cheerful efforts. So happy to continue to have designer Lucy Parissi and illustrator Qian Wu from *Tinkered Treasures* add to the beauty of this book. Gratitude for the stunning photography of Claire Richardson paired with the inspired work of stylist Nel Haynes.

Thank you to my publishing idol, Selina Lake, for providing the Foreword to this book.

Thank you to my fairy godmother Fifi O'Neill for introducing me to Cindy Richards and CICO. I will be forever grateful.

Warmest hugs to my sisters, who, like our parents, are true supporters and proud and eager listeners: Dede for her constant cheers, and Betsy for being both security blanket and compass. To my BFF Cindy for putting up with cancelled plans, and to the many dear pals at my online clubhouses (blog and Facebook) for your always uplifting comments.

Saving the best for last...thank you, thank you, thank you to my husband Jeff and our sons Jonah and Ethan for patiently indulging me while I pursue a dream that can require hours of solitude, a house with no bread, drawers without clean socks, and gems stuck to the bottom of your feet. I am forever thankful for your cheers for deadlines met and pride over finished projects. I love you with all my heart.